WEATHER

WEATHER

by Michael Cooper

Illustrated by
Mike Atkinson

GRANADA
London Toronto Sydney New York

Granada Publishing Limited
Frogmore, St Albans, Herts AL2 2NF
and
36 Golden Square, London W1R 4AH
515 Madison Avenue, New York, NY 10022, USA
117 York Street, Sydney, NSW 2000, Australia
60 International Blvd, Rexdale, Ontario R9W 6J2, Canada
61 Beach Road, Auckland, New Zealand

Published by Granada Publishing 1983

Copyright © Granada

British Library Cataloguing in Publication Data

Cooper, Michael
Weather. – (Granada guides; 40)
1. Meteorology – Juvenile literature
I. Title
551.5   QC863.5

ISBN 0 246 12059 2

Printed and bound in Great Britain by
William Collins Sons & Co Ltd, Glasgow

Granada ®
Granada Publishing ®

Contents

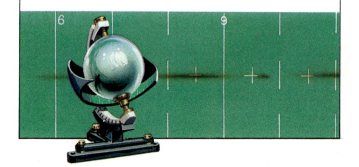

A meteorologist uses a
hand-held anemometer to
measure the wind speed high
on a mountain.

A thin layer of air surrounds
the world. This is the
atmosphere. The lower part of
the atmosphere, close to the
earth, is called the troposphere.
It is here that the clouds, winds
and other weather features are
found.

What is Weather?

Weather is the condition of the air around us at a particular time. In some parts of the world the weather is much the same day after day. In other places the weather is so variable that it is often difficult to predict even a few hours ahead. In the space of a single day, the weather may be cool, crisp and sunny in the morning, turning warm and 'muggy' with a steady drizzle by midday, then clearing in the afternoon to bring a frosty night.

The study of the weather is the science known as meteorology. Meteorologists measure, record and interpret the weather, using the results to forecast what the coming weather may be and to predict future weather patterns. They are concerned with large weather systems, such as storms, which cover huge areas and stretch far up into the atmosphere. They also study small weather systems, perhaps only a metre across or a few centimetres thick, which affect how plants and animals live.

Stratosphere
10 km

Mt Everest
8848 m

Troposphere

Weather in Myth and Magic

Our early ancestors used to think that storm clouds were the chariots of the gods and that thunder and lightning were the signs of their anger. Sailors believed that great storms at sea were caused by the sea gods, to whom they gave such names as Neptune, Triton or Poseidon. The winds were also given names, such as Zephyrus, god of the west wind. When early peoples began to farm the land they prayed to the gods for sun and rain.

In those days weather was thought magical and could only be controlled by supernatural powers. Even today some peoples still believe in the power of witch-doctors and rain makers. Others still preserve traces of early weather magic in their folklore. A stinging nettle, for instance, is thought to offer protection from lightning, and fishing boats on the Mediterranean Sea are still painted with an eye to watch for the sea gods and warn of likely storms.

Poseidon, the Ancient Greek sea god, and Boreas, god of the north wind, create a storm.

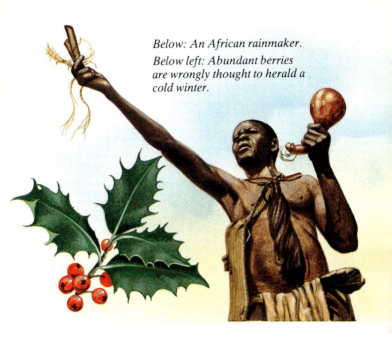

Below: An African rainmaker.

Below left: Abundant berries are wrongly thought to herald a cold winter.

In their desire to know what the weather will be, farmers and fishermen have always looked for signs in nature. Cows are said to lie down before it rains, and swallows flying high are thought to be a sign of good weather. But there is no evidence that animals sense changes in the weather before people do. Nor does there appear to be any truth in sayings which try to foretell the weather a long time ahead, such as: 'When the oak is out before the ash, then we may expect a splash'.

The only sayings which seem to have any value are those which use present weather conditions as clues to what is coming, such as: 'When the dew is on the grass, rain will never come to pass'. Cloud observation can also be useful for short term predictions. But weather lore bears no comparison with scientific forecasts.

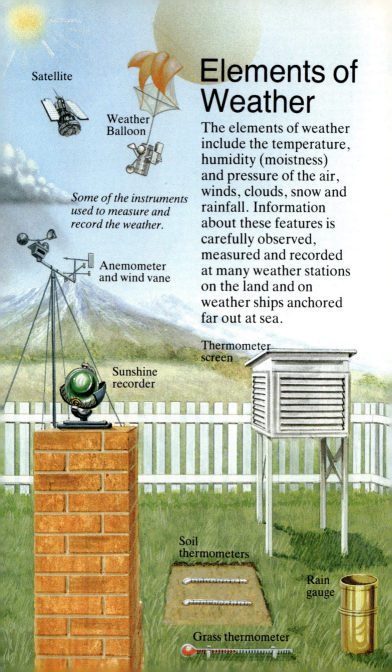

Elements of Weather

The elements of weather include the temperature, humidity (moistness) and pressure of the air, winds, clouds, snow and rainfall. Information about these features is carefully observed, measured and recorded at many weather stations on the land and on weather ships anchored far out at sea.

Satellite

Weather Balloon

Some of the instruments used to measure and record the weather.

Anemometer and wind vane

Thermometer screen

Sunshine recorder

Soil thermometers

Rain gauge

Grass thermometer

In addition, balloons are used to carry automatic measuring and transmitting devices, called radio-sondes, into the atmosphere. In recent years meteorological observation has been greatly aided by weather satellites which take photographs from space and radio the information back to earth.

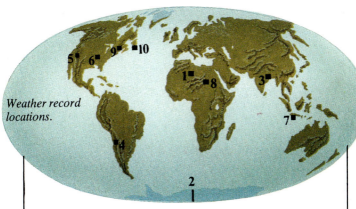

Weather record locations.

SOME WORLD WEATHER RECORDS

1 Highest temperature: 57.7°C, Libya, 1922
2 Lowest temperature: −88.3°C, Vostok, near the South Pole, 1960
3 Wettest year: 1860–61, 9299 mm at Cherrapunji, India
4 Driest year: Most years there is no rain at Calama in the Atacama desert, Chile
5 Greatest snowfall: 31.102 metres, Mt Rainier, United States, 1972

6 Biggest hailstones: 19 cm diameter, Coffeyville, Kansas, United States, 1970
7 Most thunder: 322 days a year from 1916–1919, Bogor, Java
8 Most sunshine: 4300 hours a year average, eastern Sahara desert
9 Strongest wind: 371 kph, Mt Washington, United States, 1934
10 Most fog: 120 days a year, Grand Banks, Newfoundland

Thermometers kept in a Stevenson screen record air temperatures in the shade.

Dry and wet bulb thermometers

Temperature and Humidity

The temperature of the air is measured by an ordinary mercury thermometer, sometimes called a 'dry bulb' thermometer. The humidity of the air is the amount of water vapour it contains. Humidity is measured by a hygrometer. One kind of hygrometer consists of a 'dry bulb' thermometer to measure the normal air temperature and a 'wet bulb' thermometer (the bulb is wrapped in damp material). According to the humidity of the air a certain amount of water is evaporated from the damp material – the lower the humidity the greater the evaporation. This cools the 'wet bulb' thermometer. The difference between the readings on the two thermometers is used to discover the *relative humidity* of the air (the amount of water vapour it holds compared with the amount it *could* hold at that temperature).

Pressure
and Winds

The atmosphere is held to the earth by the force of gravity, and the weight of the column of air pressing down on our head and shoulders is about one tonne, or one kilogram per square centimetre. We do not feel this great weight because our bodies are supported on all sides by an equal pressure. The pressure of the air decreases with height: at 6000 metres it is only half that at sea level.

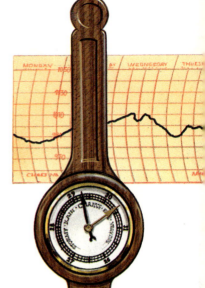

An aneroid barometer used in the home, and (behind) a barogram, a continuous record of changing pressure.

Air pressure also varies from place to place on the earth's surface. Warm air rises and expands, creating an area of low pressure, while cold, dense air sinks, creating an area of high pressure.

The pressure of the air is measured by barometers. The mercury barometer consists of a glass tube filled with mercury, sealed at one end and standing in a trough of mercury. The height of the column of mercury in the tube varies according to the pressure of the air acting on the mercury in the trough.

The aneroid barometer is the type most often seen in homes. It contains a small metal capsule out of which most of the air has been drawn. The sides of

Cold, dense air sinks and creates an area of high pressure. Warm, light air rises and creates an area of low pressure.

the capsule are held apart by a spring and move with changes in the air pressure. These movements are recorded on a dial.

Wind is simply air blowing from an area of high pressure to an area of low pressure. One way in which this happens can be seen on a summer's day at the seaside, where pressure differences build up because the land heats up and cools down more rapidly than the sea. During the day, the rapidly heated air above the land rises, creating an area of low pressure, and a current of cooler, denser air moves in from the sea to replace the rising air. This, often welcome, draught of cool air is called a sea breeze. At night the air stream is reversed as the land cools more rapidly than the sea.

The strength of the wind depends on the difference between the high and low pressure areas and the distance between them. The greater the difference and the less the distance the stronger the wind.

The speed of the wind is measured by an anemometer. One kind consists of revolving cups which are

*A wind vane and
an anemometer.*

spun by the wind and operate a speedometer. The Beaufort scale is used to classify wind strength. Numbered 0–12 it describes the wind and its notice-able effects on land. Number 6, for instance, is a fresh breeze which causes small trees in leaf to sway and flags to ripple.

The wind direction is described by the point of the compass from which the wind blows and is indicated by a wind vane which points *into* the wind. Winds which blow most often from one direction are called prevailing winds.

Three points on the Beaufort wind scale.

Dew　　　　　　　　Frost

Radiation fog

Dew, Frost and Fog

The amount of water vapour that air can hold
depends upon its temperature. The warmer the air
the more moisture it can hold in the form of invisible
vapour. Air at 20°C, for instance, can hold four times
as much water as air at 0°C. When air contains as
much water vapour as possible it is said to be
saturated, and the temperature at which this occurs
is called the dew point. If the air is cooled below this
temperature the excess water vapour condenses
(turns back to a liquid) to form water droplets.

Condensation in the air near the ground produces
fog. Water vapour which condenses on cold surfaces
forms dew or, if the temperature is low enough,
frost. Fog, dew and frost form particularly in valleys
because cold air is heavier than warm air and sinks.

Fog can form in two ways. Radiation fog occurs on
clear, cold nights when the land rapidly loses the
heat it has gained during the day and chills the air

16

lying above it. Radiation fogs are common in the autumn months. Advection fog occurs where warm, moist air moves over a cold surface. This often happens when sea air crosses a cold current or meets cold land. Smog is a mixture of fog and smoke particles which develops over industrial centres.

Dew forms when the temperature of the ground is above freezing point. Like radiation fog, it is most common in the autumn. When the temperature is below freezing point ice crystals are deposited as frost. Frost on the ground, or in fern-like patterns on window panes, is called hoar frost. Rime is clear ice which forms when very cold water droplets touch freezing objects. Trees can be festooned with rime by freezing fog or drizzle.

Mist, fog and smog. Fog is recorded if visibility is less than 1 kilometre, mist if it is less than 2 kilometres.

Clouds

Clouds are masses of small water droplets or ice crystals formed by the condensation of water vapour in rising and cooling air. Clouds have a wide variety of forms but they fall into two main types: cumuliform, or heap, clouds and stratiform, or layer, clouds. Cumuliform clouds are produced by strong rising air currents. They range from fair-weather cumulus, looking like tiny puffs of cotton-wool, to the towering, anvil-shaped cumulonimbus thunderclouds, Stratiform clouds are grey, featureless blankets which may stretch unbroken across the sky. They often form beneath a temperature inversion, where warmer air overlies cooler air. Since air will only rise above air cooler than itself, the rising currents are weak.

There is an international classification of clouds shown in the diagram opposite. They are grouped into low-, medium-, and high-level clouds according to their heights above the surface of the earth. High-level clouds are wispy and composed of ice crystals. Medium-level clouds look heavier and darker. Low-level clouds are responsible for most of our rain.

A sunshine recorder and record card.

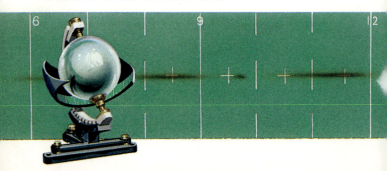

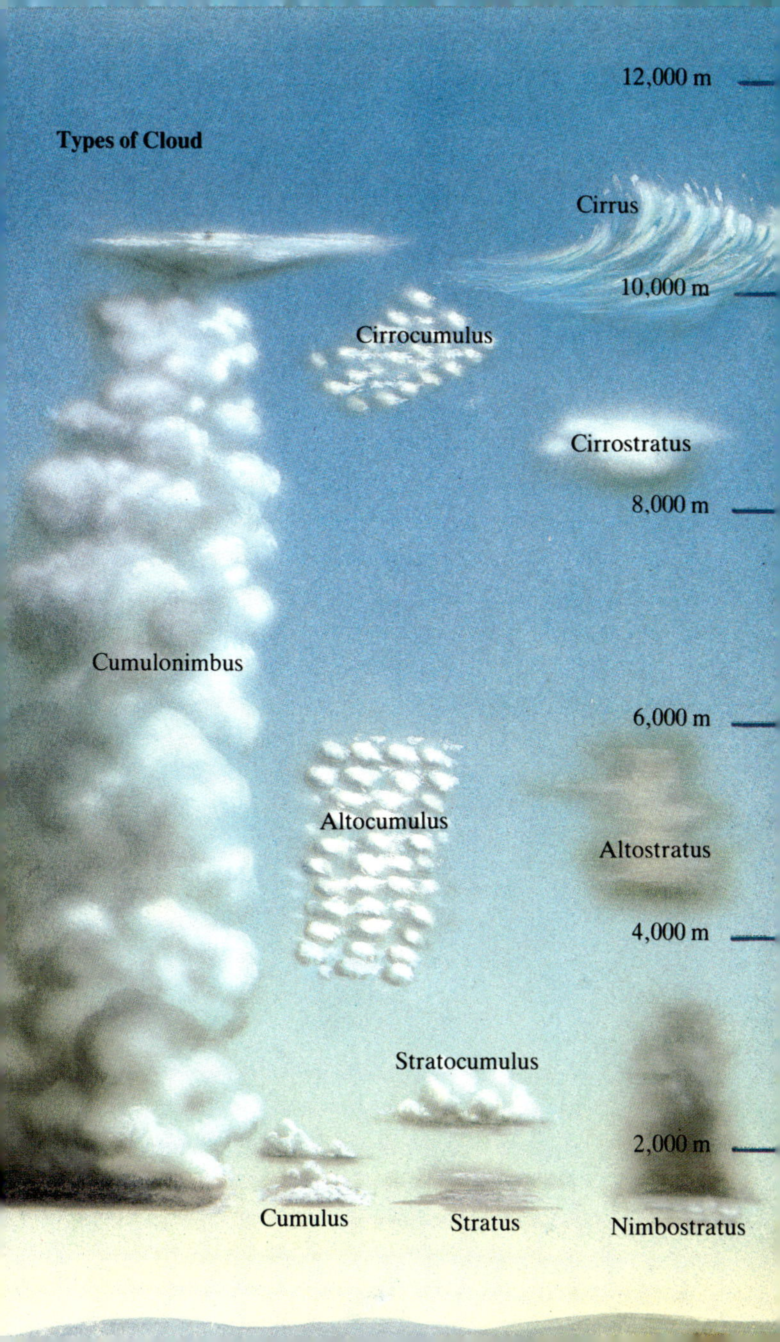

Types of Cloud

12,000 m

Cirrus

10,000 m

Cirrocumulus

Cirrostratus

8,000 m

Cumulonimbus

6,000 m

Altocumulus

Altostratus

4,000 m

Stratocumulus

2,000 m

Cumulus

Stratus

Nimbostratus

Rain and Snow

Precipitation is the name given to the rain, snow and hail which falls from clouds. As more and more water vapour condenses the cloud grows darker. The cloud droplets collide and join together until they are heavy enough to fall as rain. Hundreds of thousands of cloud droplets are needed to make one raindrop.

This is how rain forms in warm lands. In colder lands a raindrop begins its life as a tiny ice crystal. Water vapour freezes onto these ice crystals until they are heavy enough to fall from the cloud. As the ice crystals pass through warmer air at lower levels they melt and turn to raindrops. But if the air is very cold they fall as snow. Sleet is a mixture of snow and rain. Hail consists of large pellets of ice which have been tossed up and down in a thundercloud, gathering layers of ice.

A rain gauge. This type consists of a large metal canister containing a metal funnel 127 mm in diameter fitted into the top of a collecting bottle. The canister is sunk into the ground with the top 305 mm above ground level so that rainwater cannot run or bounce into it. The water from the inner collecting bottle is poured into a separate flask for measuring, generally in millimetres.

Snow crystals

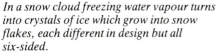

In a snow cloud freezing water vapour turns into crystals of ice which grow into snow flakes, each different in design but all six-sided.

Rain results from the rising and cooling of air. This can happen in several ways. Orographic rain occurs when air is forced to rise over mountain ranges. The rising air cools, clouds form, and rain falls over the mountain slopes. Cyclonic rain occurs in depressions (low pressure air systems) where warm air rises up over a ramp of colder air, or is lifted from the ground by a wedge of cold air. Convectional rain occurs when hot, moist air rises in strong convection currents. As the air cools, large amounts of water vapour condense and rain falls in heavy showers or thunderstorms.

Hailstones are formed of layers of ice.

Hailstones larger than tennis balls have been recorded.

21

Thunder and Lightning

Hot, sultry weather in summer is often broken by thunderstorms. A rumble of thunder is followed by a draught of cool air. Then the storm breaks, with flashes of lightning, peals of thunder, torrential rain and sometimes hail. Thunderstorms develop where hot, moist air rises rapidly in strong convection currents, or where warm air is forced aloft by cold air burrowing beneath it. Thunderstorms are most common in the tropics and over land areas with warm, moist summers. The worst storms are in lands near the equator where they occur nearly every afternoon.

Lightning is one of the most spectacular sights of nature. Sheet lightning occurs within a cloud. Forked lightning follows a zig-zag path from a cloud to the ground, or from one cloud to another.

Lightning is simply a gigantic spark of static electricity. Electricity does not normally flow through the air. It requires an electrical 'pressure' of 10,000 volts to send a spark of electricity across an air gap of one centimetre. More than 1,000,000 volts would be needed to create a flash of lightning. Scientists believe that these great electrical charges are produced by friction between the ice crystals and water droplets in the turbulent air currents.

Thunder is the sound of air expanding as it is violently heated by the lightning. We see a flash of lightning before we hear the thunder because

Metal lightning conductors protect tall buildings by providing the electricity with an easy and harmless route to the ground. The device shown above was based on the same principle.

light travels much faster than sound. It is possible to tell how far away a storm is by counting the seconds between the flash of lightning and the sound of thunder. Sound takes about 3 seconds to travel through 1 km of air.

Weather Phenomena

After a thunderstorm on 28 May 1881 hundreds of small crabs and periwinkles were found in Worcester. Once during a snowstorm in Montana snowflakes larger than tea-plates fell. Rain has been reported to fall from a clear sky and lightning has struck when no clouds were to be seen.

At times the weather does produce strange phenomena that no-one can explain but often there is a simple explanation for seemingly unnatural happenings.

Rain or snow, for example, may sometimes be coloured. It may be tinged yellow or red because it contains dust swept high into the troposphere by dust storms in the deserts and carried several thousand kilometres away.

Whirlwinds or heavy rain are probably the cause

Fireballs are strange objects not often recorded.

Strange clouds have sometimes been mistaken for space invaders.

Worms and small frogs may have appeared to 'rain' from the sky during violent downpours, but never cats and dogs.

of stories of small animals 'raining' from the sky. It rained frogs in north London on 17 August 1921. Brown worms fell from the sky one day at Clifton, Indiana and red worms at Halmstad, Sweden. All these small animals are creatures that have to keep their bodies damp. In hot, dry summer weather they hide away in damp places. As soon as a shower of rain occurs they emerge to enjoy it, and if their small bodies are blown about by the wind, then it looks as if they are coming down from the sky.

Fireballs from 100 to 200 mm in diameter, also called ball lightning, have frequently been reported. They wander slowly through the air, and some enter houses and explode, causing much damage, or pass out again through a window or up a chimney. Many people, however, do not believe that ball lightning really exists.

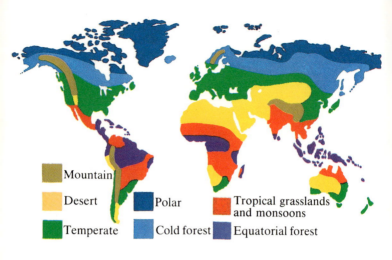

Mountain

Desert

Temperate

Polar

Cold forest

Tropical grasslands and monsoons

Equatorial forest

Weather Patterns

The lands in which people live around the world vary greatly according to the different kinds of weather they experience. These lands range from scorching deserts to icy wastes, and from dense forests to fertile valleys and grassy plains. The type and pattern of weather which these places can expect during the year is called their climate.

Near the equator the hot weather varies so little throughout the year that it is almost identical to the climate. But in the cool lands lying between latitudes 40° and 60° on the western side of the continents, the weather is so variable that the climate is difficult to describe. A broad pattern of world climates can, however, be found. This is governed by latitude and by position relative to the continents and oceans. These climatic regions may be described by the weather they experience, the natural vegetation which results, and by their location in the world.

Local conditions play an important part in modifying the weather pattern. As you go up a mountain the weather changes and a pattern of mountain climates prevails. The higher you go the colder it becomes, humidity becomes lower and atmospheric pressure decreases. Temperature and rainfall also vary greatly in a small area, and there are corresponding variations in natural plant and animal life and in human activity. Above the tree line, where it is too cold for trees to grow, there are mountain pastures and wild flowers. Above the snow line it is so cold that snow covers the ground all year. Here the sun's heat is intense because the air is thin, but the snow does not melt because it reflects the sun's rays away from it. Even at the equator high mountains may be snowcapped all year. Mountain winds blowing down the slopes warm and melt the snow lower down. In the Alps these are called Föhn winds and may cause snow avalanches.

Edelweiss

Zones of mountain weather and life.

Eagle

Saxifrage

Arctic buttercup

Bighorn

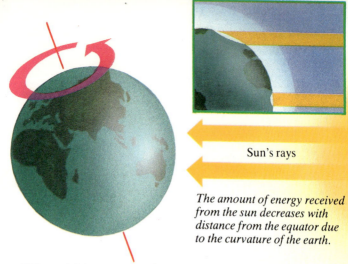

Sun's rays

The amount of energy received from the sun decreases with distance from the equator due to the curvature of the earth.

The Weather Machine

There are certain natural mechanisms which help to explain the general pattern of the world's weather. These move the air like a gigantic weather machine powered by the energy of the sun. The sun transmits its energy in the form of short-wave rays, some of which are absorbed by the earth. The earth in turn radiates this energy into the atmosphere in the form of long-wave heat rays, so warming the air. The air is hottest where most energy is received. This is at the equator and in tropical latitudes, where the sun is high in the sky. The farther away from the equator, the less the amount of energy received because of the curve of the earth's surface and atmosphere. In northern and southern lands the sun's rays are less intense because they have farther to travel through the atmosphere. They are also spread out over a greater area of the earth's surface. Consequently, temperatures are lower. Differences in temperature worldwide cause the air to circulate and to distribute the heat from the tropics to the colder regions.

The movements of the air create the earth's main surface wind belts, called the planetary winds, and the high-altitude jet streams. Heated air rises above the equator and fans out north and south. Some sinks slowly at the horse latitudes (at about 30°), from where trade winds blow towards the equator and westerlies towards the poles. Cold air sinks over the poles, causing winds to blow towards the equator. The spin of the earth deflects the winds from due northerly or southerly directions.

Surface winds are deflected by the earth's spin – to the left in the southern hemisphere, to the right in the northern hemisphere.

Circulating air creates winds near the earth's surface and jet streams high in the troposphere.

Jet streams

Surface winds

Horse latitudes

High and Low Pressure Areas

Within the tropics the sun's rays fall almost vertically on the earth's surface. The heated air expands, becomes lighter and rises. This creates an area of low pressure round the world called the doldrums. Winds blow into the doldrums to replace the rising air. These air movements are the basis of tropical weather.

In the equatorial lowlands it is like living in a hothouse. Every day temperatures rise to about 30°C because the noonday sun is almost always overhead. And there is little relief at night because the air is always humid. Early morning is the most bearable time of the day, but the sky soon clouds over and huge areas of thick cumulus cloud develop as giant spirals of rotating air carry water vapour to great

High pressure in polar regions.

High pressure in hot deserts.

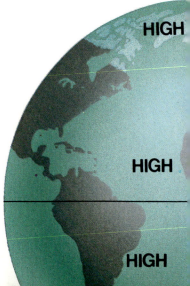

HIGH

HIGH

HIGH

heights. By late afternoon thunderstorms usually bring torrential rain which lasts into the night.

North and south of the doldrums, in the horse latitudes, cooled air descends towards the earth's surface, creating areas of permanent high pressure. The descending air fans out in a gentle spiral – in a clockwise direction in the northern hemisphere and in an anticlockwise direction in the southern hemisphere. Sometimes the weather is calm with no winds at all. Little cloud develops, so daytime temperatures are high and nights are cold. Other permanent high pressure areas occur over the poles. In these stable regions of high pressure large volumes of air develop similar characteristics of temperature and humidity. The volumes of air are referred to as air masses, and the places where they develop are called source regions.

The world's high and low pressure areas.

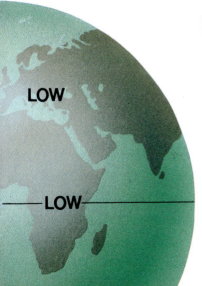

Lush forests of the equatorial low pressure regions.

Fronts and Depressions

In the temperate regions that lie between the horse latitudes and the poles the weather is very variable. Here warm, moist weather may suddenly give way to bitterly cold, dry weather. This occurs not because the air has suddenly become colder but because it has completely changed. There is a conflict in these regions between great masses of cold and warm air. As an air mass begins to move it brings changes of weather to the areas over which it passes. Moving air masses, called air streams, also change character as they move over lands or seas which are warmer or colder. The main body of an air stream brings fairly uniform conditions, but along its edge great weather changes occur.

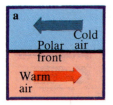 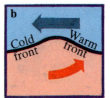 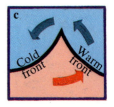

Above: A depression is born along a polar front (a). A wave forms with simple fronts (b), and winds blow round the low pressure area which develops (c), getting stronger as the depression deepens. The depression may be as much as 3,000 kilometres across and travel at about 1,000 kilometres a day. The warm air eventually rises above the cold. The front is then said to be occluded, and the depression dies.

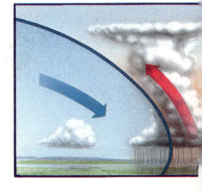

Where the cold and warm air streams approach each other or move alongside each other, the air will not mix. The edges, or fronts, of these different kinds of air become the scene of those great changes that sweep across the mid-latitude regions in the form of depressions. These weather systems form where warm air edges into the cold air and rises above it along a warm front. Cold air moving against the warm air cuts beneath it along a cold front. The water vapour in the rising warm air condenses to create belts of rain cloud. Along the fronts the winds are said to back and veer as they change direction.

Smaller weather systems which also develop in these regions are ridges of high pressure, which bring short periods of settled weather, and troughs of low pressure, which bring rain.

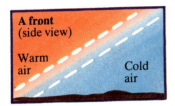

A front
(side view)

Warm air

Cold air

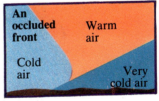

An occluded front

Warm air

Cold air

Very cold air

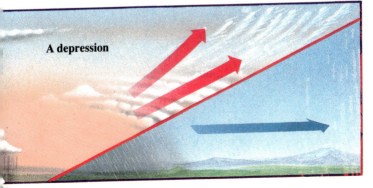

A depression

The Seasons

Why does spring come to melt the winter snow? The rhythm of the seasons is caused by the tilt of the spinning earth at an angle of about 23½° from the vertical to its path round the sun. This tilt points first one hemisphere then the other towards the sun.

The earth's tilt means that the zone receiving the greatest amount of heat from the sun changes through the year. It varies from the Tropic of Cancer in the north (June) to the Tropic of Capricorn in the south (December).

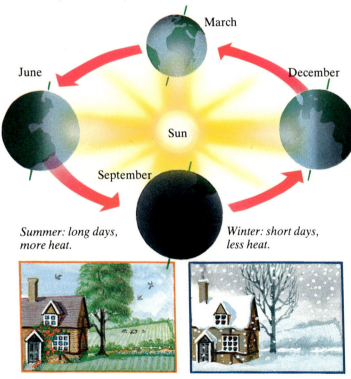

March

June

December

Sun

September

Summer: long days, more heat.

Winter: short days, less heat.

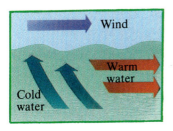
Ocean currents in the Atlantic redistribute heat and cold, influencing the air masses that pass over them.

Wind

Warm water

Cold water

Ocean Currents

The complex workings of the oceans and the weather machine affect each other. The oceans heat and cool more slowly than the land. Consequently, they are a cooling influence in summer and a warming influence in winter in those coastal lands where there would otherwise be a great difference between summer and winter temperatures.

Ocean currents also affect the climate of coastal lands. Some are cold, others are warm, and their pattern is complex. They are formed chiefly by winds moving the surface waters, which are then replaced by cold waters from the ocean depths. Cold currents lower the temperature of neighbouring lands and cause advection fogs, such as those that beset San Francisco, California. Dense fogs in the north-west Atlantic are caused when warm winds cross the cold Labrador current. In northwest Europe warm waters moving from the tropics in the Gulf Stream keep northern ports free of winter ice, and winds carry the warmth inland.

The Water Cycle

When you watch rain falling, a stream flowing or a plant or animal living and growing, you are observing part of the earth's water cycle. Also called the hydrological cycle, this is the never-ending process of nature in which water from the oceans is constantly passing into the atmosphere, down to the land and then back to the oceans again. The heat from the sun evaporates about 15 million tonnes of moisture from the earth's surface every second. Some of the water, which falls back as rain or snow, may take a long time to return to the oceans. Some may evaporate again directly from the land or from the leaves of plants through transpiration. A bottle garden is a miniature example of the way water is recycled on earth and in the atmosphere.

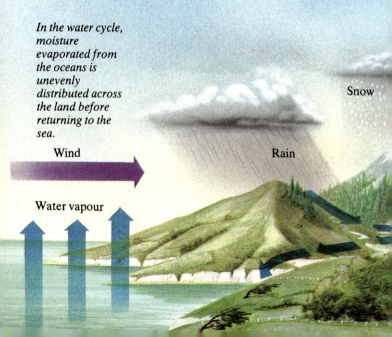

In the water cycle, moisture evaporated from the oceans is unevenly distributed across the land before returning to the sea.

Snow

Wind

Rain

Water vapour

It has been estimated that there are about 1400 million cubic kilometres of water in the world and that about 97 per cent is always in the oceans. The remaining 3 per cent maintains the water cycle. Three-quarters of this is locked in the earth's glaciers and ice sheets. Most of the rest is in the rocks, soils, rivers and lakes. Only 0.035 per cent is in the atmosphere. This is enough to give all the land areas 900–1,000 mm of rainfall in a year. However, the rain is by no means evenly distributed over the earth.

In the equatorial lowlands there is heavy convectional rain every day. In contrast, India is in the path of the seasonal southwest monsoon, a wind bringing torrential rain, followed by a season of dry weather and often prolonged drought. Deserts such as the Gobi in Asia are deep within the continents, far from the moisture-laden winds. Other dry areas may lie in the rain shadow of high mountains where the winds are warming and drying as they descend.

A bottle garden, a water cycle in miniature.

Wind

Rain shadow

Scrub and desert

Shaping the Land

Scree formed by frost shattering.

Soil formed from chalk.

The weather can vary greatly between places only a short distance apart. On a hot day, for example, people can escape the heat of the city in the cooler surrounding countryside. There are also other variations, and much attention is paid by meteorologists to the layer of air close to the ground in which life is most abundant. This branch of the science is called micrometeorology.

Flood waters spread rock particles over a plain, and soils form, supporting cool, green vegetation.

Micrometeorology helps to explain how the weather attacks our surroundings. Rocks, for instance, are shattered by frost or dissolved away as dew and rain remove the chemicals in them. In deserts the heat of the sun by day and the cold of the night causes the rocks to expand and contract so much that layers split off and water and wind carry the fragments away. Wind blown sand cuts into other rocks, wearing them into strange shapes. The wind piles the sand into dunes, and in dust storms it may blow the finest particles far away.

In cities, buildings are slowly destroyed by the weather, but they also create their own weather conditions. According to their colour and texture they reflect varying amounts of heat. And according to their design they can change the wind direction, causing swirling gusts and eddies.

The strange landscapes of hot, barren deserts are largely the result of wind erosion.

Weather Long Ago

Not only does the weather fluctuate from day to day, but also the climate produced by the weather undergoes changes, though over longer periods of time. The study of the climates and weather patterns of the past helps us to understand our present weather. Long-term patterns of change have a rhythm extending over hundreds of thousands of years. Evidence for their existence lies in the rocks and in the story of life on earth. Geologists can trace the story of ancient climates from the fossils of animals and plants left in the rocks. The rocks themselves may consist, for example, of ancient river sediments and sand dunes. There may even be evidence of the weather itself from traces of sudden storms or of wind ripples in the sand.

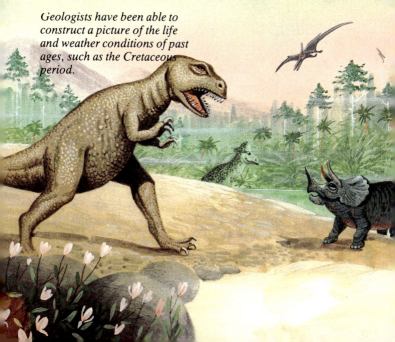

Geologists have been able to construct a picture of the life and weather conditions of past ages, such as the Cretaceous period.

Mammoths lived on the snowy plains of Europe and Asia during the Ice Age.

Because the great land masses of the earth are moving about, they have experienced great climatic changes. Places where coal is found today must once have been near the equator, for coal is the remains of tropical swamp forests. And places where ice caps once existed must have been near the poles.

All the evidence points to the fact that we are living in an ice age. Ice ages last for several million years, during which time the ice sheets ebb and flow. But they are rare events in the story of the earth. For most of the earth's history ocean currents have carried warmth from the equator to the poles. Today this is not possible; the moving land masses have shut off the Arctic Ocean and the icy continent of Antarctica surrounds the south pole. This has helped to create the conditions necessary for an ice age.

Future Weather

Scientists know from the study of past weather that we are living in a warm phase during an ice age. Great ice sheets have advanced and retreated four times over much of northern Europe. Between these glacial periods the climate grew so warm that hippopotamuses wallowed in the rivers and elephants roamed the land. One day the ice sheets may return but it is not likely to happen for a long time. The last warm phase lasted for some 50,000 years: the present warm phase began only 10,000 years ago.

Whether or not the ice sheets return, there are many less dramatic changes in the climate. Only 200 years ago the rivers of western Europe, such as the Thames, which do not freeze today, were regularly frozen over. And within recorded history the Sahara was a much smaller desert.

Climatic changes probably result from variations in the amount of heat the earth receives from the sun. There are many possible explanations for this. The path of the earth around the sun may become more elliptical, or the tilt of the planet's axis may change. In both cases winters would become colder and summers warmer.

People may also be helping to change the climate. The burning of fuels such as coal, oil and petrol is increasing the amount of carbon dioxide in the air. Carbon dioxide is largely responsible for trapping the heat radiated by the earth and even small increases in the amount may be enough to increase the world's temperatures slightly. It has been estimated that an overall increase of only 2°C would be sufficient to melt the ice caps and flood low-lying plains.

The wobble of the earth on its axis and the amount of dust in the atmosphere will affect the future weather.

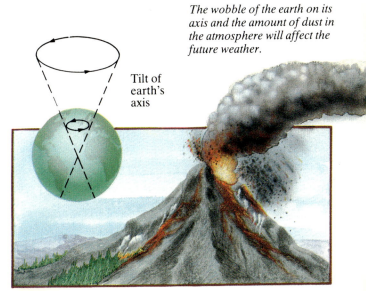

Tilt of earth's axis

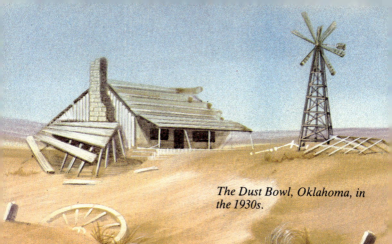

The Dust Bowl, Oklahoma, in the 1930s.

Weather Disasters

The weather is responsible for many natural disasters. Extremes of heat and cold may kill crops and livestock, bringing ruin to farmers. Storms cause rivers and seas to flood the land, while hurricane-force winds destroy everything in their path.

Some places are more liable to extremes of weather than others: hurricane damage, for instance, is confined to coastal lands, and the worst droughts occur on the margins of deserts. But freak conditions can cause havoc almost anywhere at any time.

In some cases people themselves have created the conditions which have resulted in disaster. The American Dust Bowl was created by farmers ploughing dry grasslands. Strong winds blew away the fine topsoil from whole farms overnight. In Holland large floods have occurred when storm waves have breached the dykes built to reclaim land from the sea.

SOME NOTABLE WEATHER DISASTERS

1900 Storm tide leaves 6,000 dead along the coast of Texas, U.S.

1906 Typhoon strikes Hong Kong, killing 50,000 people.

1911 Yangtze River, China, floods, causing 100,000 deaths.

1925 Tornadoes in central U.S. claim 700 lives in one day

1931 Yangtze River, China, floods, drowning 150,000 people

1953 Storm tides claim 2,000 lives along the shores of the North Sea.

1955 Hurricane causes some £1 billion of damage along the eastern coast of the U.S. but fewer than 200 deaths.

1962 Avalanche in Peru buries more than 3,000 people

1963 Cyclone and tidal waves leave 20,000 dead in East Pakistan.

1966 Arno River floods Florence, Italy, destroying priceless works of art.

1970 Cyclone kills half a million people in East Pakistan

1975 Drought in northeastern Africa leads to famine in which some 50,000 die.

Heavy snowfalls may bring cities to a temporary standstill but in rural areas they can spell disaster to livestock.

Too Little Water

Many areas of the world suffer from unexpected droughts. The great Californian drought of 1976–77 was one of the worst on record in the United States. Holiday business and cold drink sales boomed, but farmers suffered and the price of food in the shops increased. There were droughts at the same time in Europe, and water had to be rationed in Britain as the reservoirs dried up.

In some parts of the world droughts have become persistent. A belt of drought from the Sahel region of West Africa, through Ethiopia to northwest India has caused widespread starvation. Scientists who have studied the weather patterns of the Sahel think that the world's climates may be shifting. Together with the use of farming methods not suited to this drier weather, this is causing the desert to spread farther south into former grassland regions.

Drought in the Sahel, Africa

Water-
Vital
Resource
For Life

A poster stresses the importance of adequate rainwater.

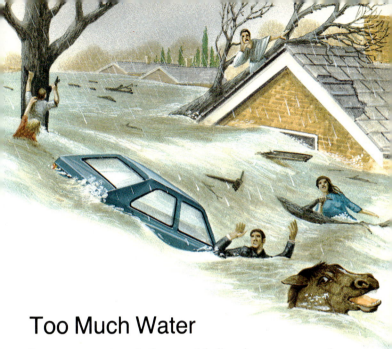

Too Much Water

In some parts of the world floods are a regular, though always alarming, happening, wasting water that may be badly needed at other times or in other places. Torrential rains brought by the monsoon wind in 1978 caused the worst river floods for 100 years in India. One person in twenty was affected, 15,000 drowned, and more than 500,000 homes were destroyed.

Floods are common events worldwide, but only severe ones are newsworthy. When Florence, in Italy, was flooded in 1966 volunteers from many countries arrived to save the art treasures ruined by mud and oil. The 1976–77 droughts in California and Europe were then followed by serious floods. Rain and snow blocked passes in the Alps in the summer, Moscow was flooded, and heavy rain ruined the Soviet grain harvest.

Hurricanes and Tornadoes

Eye

Vortex   Tail

A hurricane, seen from above.

Hurricanes are the greatest of all storms. The energy they contain is far greater than that of a hydrogen bomb explosion. Hurricanes are also known in different parts of the world as tropical cyclones, typhoons and willy-willies.

Hurricanes are born in the tropics during the late summer when the heat of the sun evaporates large amounts of water from the sea. The hot, moist air rises and condenses to form cumulus cloud. The process of condensation releases heat and the air continues to rise. Winds sweep in to fill the void left by the rising air and create a whirlpool of air spiralling inward, ever faster, towards the centre of low pressure. In the vortex they may reach speeds of 320 kph, but at the central 'eye' of the storm the air is still and clear.

Hurricanes often devastate Caribbean islands and the Gulf coast of the United States, where huge waves 8–9 metres high, called hurricane surges, swamp the coastal areas. In November 1970 at least 500,000 people died when a hurricane surge reached the mouth of the River Ganges in Bangladesh, and in 1974 the city of Darwin, Australia, was devastated.

A tornado is more violent than a hurricane, but is smaller. As clouds condense, a funnel of air is sucked up into the sky. Over the sea this forms a water spout. Winds whirl at up to 800 kph as the funnel follows a meandering path, perhaps 400 metres wide, leaving a swathe of damage behind.

Tornadoes cause great damage. They are common on the Great Plains of the United States, where they are known as twisters.

Weather Forecasts

The word 'forecast' was first used by Britain's Chief Meteorologist, Admiral Fitzroy, in 1850 to give a more scientific image to the new methods of predicting the weather. Today specialized forecasts are issued for many purposes. Forecasts of wet spells are of special concern to farmers or the organizers of outdoor events. Detailed briefings are given to aircraft navigators, and fog, frost and snow warnings are sent to motoring organizations and ships. Especially hazardous conditions are carefully monitored, for example by the United States Meteorological Service 'Storm Watch' to predict the formation of hurricanes.

Because the weather is a global force, successful forecasting must be organized on a worldwide scale. Most countries are members of the World Meteorological Organization, which has established the World Weather Watch. This is beginning to enable more accurate short-term weather forecasts to be made. It is also making possible predictions of the

Storm warnings are a vital part of weather forecasting and can help to save lives.

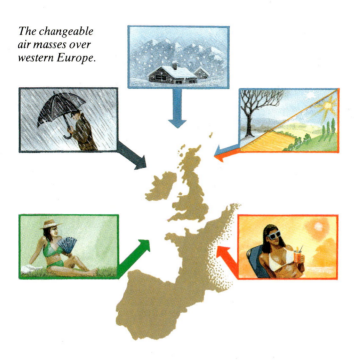

The changeable air masses over western Europe.

long-term weather patterns and climate changes which help scientists to plan the future use of farmland, fuel and other resources.

Some phenomena, however, such as tornadoes and thunderstorms, develop so quickly that they may only be forecast a short time ahead. Attempts to make detailed long-range forecasts a month ahead have not been very successful. Seasonal forecasts, however, are more successful. They involve studies of the ocean currents and their temperatures and of the way the jet streams swing the warm or cold air masses north or south, especially over the western parts of Europe and the United States.

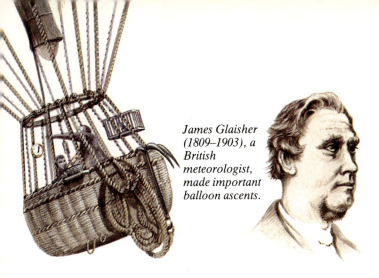

James Glaisher (1809–1903), a British meteorologist, made important balloon ascents.

Weather forecasting was not possible until instruments were invented to measure the atmosphere and assemble the information quickly so that the pattern could be interpreted before the weather arrived. The Ancient Greeks were interested in explaining the weather. The study of weather was called meteorology after Aristotle's book on the atmosphere entitled *Meteorologica*. But meteorology only became a science when the barometer was invented in 1643 by the physicist Evangelista Torricelli. Nobody knew then why air pressure varied, although it was seen to be linked to the weather processes. Galileo experimented with a thermoscope to measure air temperature in 1593, but the first thermometer suitable for general use was the mercury thermometer introduced in 1657.

It was not until the telegraph was developed in 1844 that it became possible to assemble the weather records necessary to make weather charts from information gathered on the same day. From 1855 onwards countries all over the world began to organ-

52

ize their observations at specific hours. For quicker transmission, mathematical codes were used which have developed into internationally accepted ways of sending weather messages.

Information about the upper atmosphere is crucial for understanding the weather. As early as 1749 kites were used to carry thermometers, and after the Montgolfier brothers invented the hot air balloon, an ascent to 2,740 metres was made to measure temperature, humidity and pressure. James Glaisher made important balloon ascents to obtain data between 1862 and 1866, reaching 3,700 metres without supplies of oxygen. In 1937 the first unmanned balloons carrying meteorological instruments and radio transmitters were made in Britain. By the late 1940s it was possible to get a true picture not only of the weather patterns at the earth's surface but also of the air movements high above, and the information could be transmitted without delay.

Television brings weather forecasts to a large public.

Gathering Weather Information

In recent years a number of technical advances have helped meteorologists to collect weather information. Data is gathered from many land stations, weather ships, ocean-going vessels and aircraft. In many parts of the world there are automatic weather stations which provide information from polar regions, deserts and other places where few people live and where manned weather stations would be difficult and expensive to run. Some of these stations are anchored to buoys in the sea.

Radar can be used to locate showers, rain belts, thunderstorms and hurricanes because the water droplets they contain reflect short-wave radio signals. The size, position and direction of these features is shown on a screen, the centre of which marks the position of the observer.

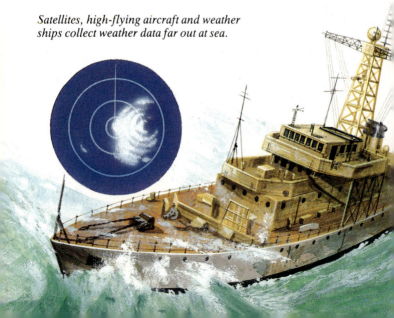

Satellites, high-flying aircraft and weather ships collect weather data far out at sea.

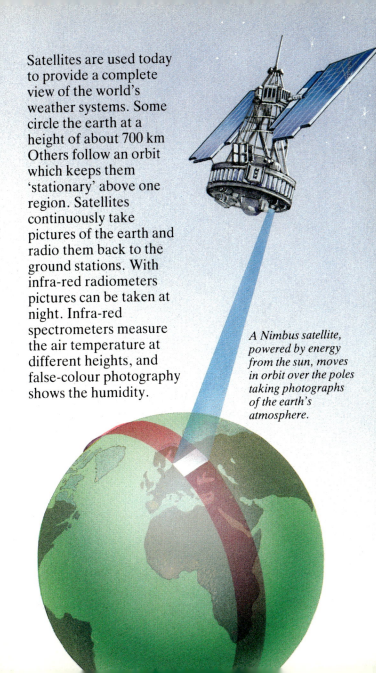

Satellites are used today to provide a complete view of the world's weather systems. Some circle the earth at a height of about 700 km Others follow an orbit which keeps them 'stationary' above one region. Satellites continuously take pictures of the earth and radio them back to the ground stations. With infra-red radiometers pictures can be taken at night. Infra-red spectrometers measure the air temperature at different heights, and false-colour photography shows the humidity.

A Nimbus satellite, powered by energy from the sun, moves in orbit over the poles taking photographs of the earth's atmosphere.

The Synoptic Chart

Weather information is collected from the various observers scattered around the world at fixed times called synoptic hours. It is first sent to regional stations and then to major centres, such as the British Meteorological Office in Bracknell, where a 24-hour forecast can be prepared from it in a few minutes. The details are exchanged between countries four times every day, at midnight, 06.00, 12.00 and 18.00 hours Greenwich Mean Time. Teleprinters pour out millions of reports each day.

With the information also coming in from satellites, this vast amount of detail would be unmanageable without high-speed computers. Reports are translated into a sequence of numbers, used internationally, in groups of five figures. These are used to construct mathematical representations of the atmosphere at various levels.

Synoptic charts are made from the coded records.

The weather details provided by each station are shown around a station model, as it is called, some in the numbered code and some as symbols. Isobars, which are lines joining places with the same air pressure, are also shown on the chart and numbered in millibars. Warm fronts are indicated along their leading edge by semicircles, cold fronts by triangles, and occluded fronts by alternating semicircles and triangles.

Human experience and judgement also play their part and turn the computer forecast into words and simplified maps for the benefit of the general public.

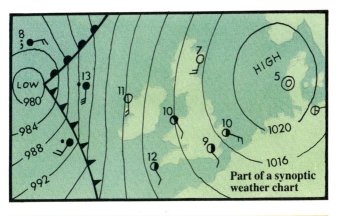

Part of a synoptic weather chart

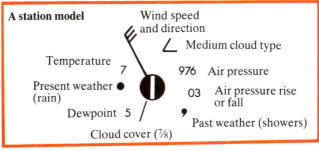

A station model

Wind speed and direction

Medium cloud type

Temperature 7

Present weather ● (rain)

Dewpoint 5

Cloud cover (⅞)

976 Air pressure

03 Air pressure rise or fall

Past weather (showers)

Controlling the Weather

The idea of controlling the weather is an age-old dream which is still a long way off, but there is much interest today in the possibilities of at least modifying the weather. The United States government has funded many research projects, such as 'Skywater' to increase snowfall in the mountains, 'Skyfire' to suppress lightning, and 'Stormfury' to control hurricanes.

The art of weather modification, which is still in its infancy, began in the mid 1940s, when it was found that dry ice stimulated snowfall when scattered over clouds in Massachusetts. The ice provided the small particles, or nuclei, necessary for the snow to form.

Protecting crops from hail in China, one of the more successful aspects of weather modification.

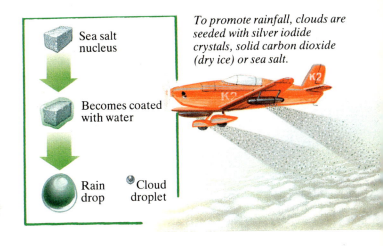

Sea salt nucleus

Becomes coated with water

Rain drop

Cloud droplet

To promote rainfall, clouds are seeded with silver iodide crystals, solid carbon dioxide (dry ice) or sea salt.

In the same way, seeding clouds with various other substances creates the nuclei needed to promote rainfall. Clouds lacking suitable nuclei can cool as low as −20°C without precipitation.

Hailstorms cause immense damage to crops, so in the Soviet Union and China hail clouds are bombarded with anti-hail shells filled with chemicals. These provide nuclei around which only tiny hailstones form, so they turn to rain as they fall. Seeding hurricanes to reduce their intensity, however, has met with varying degrees of success. The aim is to increase the eye of the hurricane by seeding around it with soot. There are many dangers in such experiments. In 1947 a seeded hurricane off the United States changed course, causing extensive damage in Georgia. Also, cloud seeding in Australia and elsewhere has caused floods and crop damage in places where rain was not intended. In many places there is a ban on weather modification.

Solar panel

Windbreak of poplar trees

Wind fan in orchard

Plant conservatory

Much weather modification is possible on a small scale around the home.

On a small scale the weather can be modified considerably. Artificial temperatures and humidities can be created, for instance, in glasshouses so that tropical plants can be grown in colder lands. Homes can be air-conditioned to provide pleasant temperatures all year round, and in some towns shopping precincts are built with climate-control systems. The sun's energy itself can be trapped by solar panels to provide warmth and the electric power needed for these modifications. Windbreaks can be used to protect homes and crops, as in the Rhône Valley in southern France, where rows of poplar trees are grown as protection against the Mistral wind. To prevent the formation of fog, the air around airport runways is often heated, and in Florida pots of burning oil and large electric fans warm and move the air to prevent frost damaging the fruit crops. Irrigation, used worldwide to provide water for plant roots, also creates the necessary humidity for healthy plant growth near ground level.

Everywhere people's activities affect the weather by altering the clarity of the air and the physical surface of the ground. Many of the modifications have been inadvertent. When valleys are flooded, marshes drained, forests cleared and planted, and the chemical composition of the air altered by factory smoke and traffic fumes, the temperature and humidity of the air and the direction and force of the wind are all affected. Buildings also deflect winds and create islands of warmth, especially at night, as they retain heat.

Increasingly, people are becoming aware of the need to make positive use of their ability to modify the weather as well as to prevent the undesirable effects of their activities on local weather systems.

Large reservoirs and newly planted forests modify local conditions and help to maintain the global balance of the atmosphere.

Index